CARING FOR SOMEBODY ELSE'S KIDS!

TOP TIPS AND ADVICE TO CARE FOR SOMEBODY ELSE'S KIDS

By

DAVE CREWE

ABOUT THE AUTHOR

Dave Crewe has been a qualified Social Worker since 1995. Prior to this he worked in Probation and in the field of Drug and Alcohol abuse. Since 1995 Dave has worked in Children's Services within a number of Local Authorities, the main one being the Isle of Wight.

He has a wide knowledge and experience of many aspects of the social work role, including; Child Protection, Assessment, Looked After Children and Fostering and Adoption. He has worked as a Social Worker, Team Manager and latterly as a Group Manager for children in care.

Since 2011 Dave has also worked as a Professional Advisor and Manager to both Fostering and Adoption Panels across the Country.

More recently, Dave has managed Fostering teams, LAC teams and has developed a pan Dorset Private Fostering Service that is commissioned by other Local Authorities.

It was while working in Fostering and with looked after children that Dave became aware that there was a lack of resources available to foster carers (particularly new ones) that would provide them with straightforward, practical advice on day to day issues that arise when caring for other people's children. Issues that may not be serious enough to call the social worker, but where they need a little advice and guidance. That's why he decided to write this book.

This book is not meant to be an encyclopedia of childcare strategies, nor is it intended to be read from cover to cover in order of chapters. It is intended as a handy book of advice, tips and hints that you can quickly refer to when you are not sure what to do in specific circumstances

It is written in a light hearted, informal style despite the seriousness of the subject matter. Dave intended this book to be readable, enjoyable and informative, but not too heavy! If you want a serious, academic volume on childcare, then you had better look elsewhere, as this is not it!

As a foster carer or adopter you are on an exciting and often eventful journey...so let that journey begin!

Dave can be contacted at:

davecrewe@yahoo.com

http://www.davecrewe.co.uk

TABLE OF CONTENTS

INTRODUCTION

So, you have been on the courses and the Prep Groups, you've been to Panel, you've had a grilling and now you are ready to care for somebody else's child! This is where the hard work begins...where the rubber meets the road!

It may seem daunting (and sometimes it is!), but you can do it. You will have the support of Social Workers and other professionals every step of the way, but what about when they have all gone home and the offices are closed? What about those situations where you don't want to bother other professionals because it's not a big issue or you don't want to appear to be out of your depth? Well that is where this little book comes in. You can dip in and out of it depending on the situation at hand. It is packed with useful tips, advice and strategies to help you on your journey caring for other people's children. Sometimes it's the same as caring for your own children....and most of the time... it isn't!

The important thing is, if you are unsure about something, always discuss it with your support worker or the child's social worker.

You will also notice that throughout the book I have referred to your "foster child". This is just for convenience and ease of reading. All of the tips and advice in this book can be applied to adopted children, your own children or even children that you childmind.

Anyway, enough of my waffling, I'm sure that you are eager to get into the main chapters of the book and to start learning some new stuff (and be reminded of some stuff that you already know!). The one thing that I would say though is that none of the advice, tips and strategies in this book will work unless you put them into practice! You must take action...that's when the magic happens...

CHAPTER 1

YOUR EVER CHANGING ROLE AS A FOSTER CARER

You watch your foster children grow right before your very eyes. It seems like yesterday they were learning to crawl, walk, and feed themselves, and now they're in school, involved in activities, making friends, and learning to be more and more independent. Foster Carers have said that from the time they're placed, they are constantly learning to let go. As a result, your parenting strategies have to change. As your foster child grows, develops, learns, and matures, so does your foster caring role.

As your foster child has grown, you undoubtedly have discovered that they have their own unique personality and temperament. You've probably unconsciously redeveloped your parenting skills around the individual needs of your foster child. And no two children are exactly alike, and therefore, your parenting style shouldn't be either. Some foster children may need more guidance and feel more unsure of themselves, so you may have become used to having to guide, lead, show and encourage that child consistently through their childhood while still trying to encourage independence and give praise in order to build their self-esteem and confidence levels. Another child may be very intrinsically motivated and very willful and not need a great deal of guidance or leadership from you. While you encourage their independence, it's also important that you also encourage their ability to ask for help when needed and continue to praise good deeds, actions, and traits.

The most important tools you have in order to successfully adjust your parenting/caring skills are your eyes and your ears. You have to see what's going on with your foster child and you have to hear what they are telling you. It's important that you encourage your foster child to be their own individual, while still being available to them at whatever level or degree they need you to be. Sometimes it's situation-specific as well. A foster child may not need you to be as directly involved with their schooling to ensure their overall academic success, but they may need you to be more involved in their social life as they may be feeling a bit shaky or scared when it comes to making new friends or meeting new people.

So the bottom line is this: as your foster child grows and changes, so should your parenting skills. Keep your eyes and ears open and communicate honestly and openly with your foster child, and you'll both mature gracefully.

15

PROVIDING A SAFE AND SECURE HOME FOR YOUR FOSTER CHILD

Accidents in the home are the primary cause of injuries in children. By taking a few simple precautions, these injuries can be avoided, making your home safe for your foster child and the other children who visit it.

In your kitchen, you should be sure to install safety latches on cabinets and drawers. This helps keep children away from the everyday household chemicals you use to clean your home and dishes with and also keeps them from grabbing sharp objects like scissors or knives from inside the drawers. Use the back burners when cooking on the stove and keep the handles of your pots and pans turned out of a curious child's reach while cooking.

Safety latches should be installed on cabinets and drawers in your bathrooms, as well, to keep them away from unsafe household cleaning products and medicines. Be sure to unplug any electrical appliances, such as hair dryers or curling tongs, directly after use, and put them out of a child's reach.

Teach your foster children early on that electricity and water do not mix and that no electrical appliances of any kind should ever be immersed in or placed under running water. Toilet locks should also be used in homes that have small children to keep lids down. Young children are 'top heavy' and can easily fall into a toilet if they lean in to play in it. Since a young child can drown in less than an inch of water, it is imperative to closely supervise them in the bathroom at all times.

Around your house, be sure to secure furniture, such as bookshelves and heavy furniture that could tip easily, to the wall using brackets. Use doorknob covers to keep children out of rooms with potential hazards and to keep them from leaving the house unsupervised. Make sure your window blinds do not have looped cords on them, as they can present a strangulation hazard to a young child. And always cover your electrical outlets with protective covers to keep small fingers from them and small objects from being inserted into them.
Check your house over regularly for other potential hazards and address them immediately. You should also undertake an annual Health and Safety check with your Fostering Support Worker. With these precautions and some common sense, your household will be your foster child's haven.

Chapter 2

SELF ESTEEM

It has often been said that children learn what they live. So if you're looking for a place to start helping your foster child to build positive self-esteem and self-value, then you should show them your positive sense of self and strong self-esteem. Be positive when you speak about yourself and highlight your strengths. This will teach your foster child that it's okay to be proud of their talents, skills and abilities.

Your foster child also benefits greatly from honest and positive praise. Find something about them to praise each day. You could even give your foster child a task you know they can complete and then praise them for a job well done after they're finished. Show your foster child that positive acts merit positive praise.

When your foster child is feeling sad, angry or depressed, communicate openly, honestly and patiently with them. Listen to them without judging or criticizing. They may not fully understand why they feel the way they do, so the opportunity to communicate with you about it may be what is needed to help them sort through a difficult situation. Suggest positive behaviours and options as solutions, and make sure to leave that door of communication open so they know the next time they feel bad, they can come to you for help and know that you won't judge or punish them for how they're feeling.

Teach your foster child the importance of setting goals and developing a plan to meet that goal and complete that task. Small projects are the best to start off with in the beginning. Ensure that it's an appropriate task for your foster child, and not too complex. Don't only give praise at the end of the project, but praise their accomplishments during the project as well.

Most importantly, tell your child "I care about you" each and every day - many times throughout the day, in fact. When they've behaved badly, remind yourself that it's not them that you don't like, only their behaviour. Tuck short, sweet notes in their lunchboxes or coat pockets, or even send them a card in the mail. Soon, they'll learn to say "I care about you" just as easily and honestly in return.

BUILDING A HEALTHY SENSE OF SELF ESTEEM

Your foster child's self-esteem is their mental foundation. A self-assured foster child is confident, secure, happy, well-adjusted and successful. They can solve problems that come their way, and thrive under a foster carer's nurturing care.

What are some good ways to build self-esteem in your foster child?
Most importantly, accept your foster child for who they are, and help them to do the same. Teach your foster child that nobody is perfect, and that everyone makes mistakes. Show them how to learn and grow from their mistakes, and let them know that you also make mistakes. Children with high self-esteem are able to take lessons from mistakes and apply them down the road. A foster child with low self-esteem becomes frustrated and resorts to self-depreciating behaviour, such as calling themselves 'stupid' and vowing to 'never try that again.'
Help your foster child discover their abilities and talents, and encourage outlets for them to build on

and improve them. Praise a foster child not only for improvements in abilities and skills, but also for the traits they naturally possess.

Encourage your foster child to make positive choices. Open an honest dialog with your foster child and discuss the possibilities with them. Children who learn skills for making positive choices when they are younger are well-prepared for the tougher choices they have to make when they are older.

Ensure that you spend lots of quality time with your foster child, at least once a week. Whether you are kicking a football, drawing pictures or going out to grab a hamburger, take time to talk and keep in touch.

If you find it difficult to squeeze in quality time during a hectic week, take the time to talk about things during the drive to school or while they are helping you put the groceries away.

ENCOURAGE YOUR FOSTER CHILD TO FEEL IMPORTANT

It's imperative for any child's healthy development to feel important and worthy. Healthy self-esteem is a child's armour against the challenges of the world. Children who feel good about themselves seem to have an easier time handling conflicts and resisting negative pressures. They tend to smile more readily and enjoy life. These children are realistic and generally optimistic. It has also been shown that children who feel important are well-rounded, respectful, and excel in academics, extra-curricular activities and hobbies, and develop healthy relationships with their peers.

In contrast, children who do not feel important or cherished have low self-esteem, and challenges can become sources of major anxiety and frustration. Children who think poorly of themselves have a hard time solving problems, and may become passive, withdrawn, or depressed.

You are the biggest influence on your foster child feeling important, valued and worthy. Remember to praise your foster child for a job well done, and also for putting in a good effort. Praise the good traits they naturally possess, and help them find ways to learn from their mistakes and failures. Be honest and sincere in your praise. Help them realise that you also suffer from self-doubt and can make mistakes from time to time, but that you know that you are important, valued and loved. When you nurture your own self-esteem and importance, your foster child will learn to do the same, so be sure to lead by example and steer clear of self-depreciating yourself or engaging in activities that lower your self-worth or importance. Your foster child may have inaccurate or irrational beliefs about themselves, their abilities or their traits. Accentuate the positive about your foster child, and encourage your foster child to set realistic expectations and standards for themselves. Help them identify traits or skills they would like to improve and help them come up with a game plan for accomplishing that goal. Encourage your foster child to become involved in cooperative activities that foster a sense of teamwork and accomplishment.

Through these and other positive, affirming activities, your foster child is sure to develop a strong sense of self-importance, value and worth which will carry into their adult years.

Positive Praise

Praising a foster child correctly is important to the development of positive behaviours. It's a great way to encourage constructive future behaviour. When you give praise, you are giving your foster child a feeling of positive feedback, which increases their sense of confidence, self-esteem and abilities. When you praise your foster child, you are pointing out the way they've acted, an action they've taken, or simply who they are. When your foster child looks good, tell them so. When your foster child does anything that pleases you, let them know. You should also praise a foster child's effort to do well, even if it doesn't come out so good in the end. You should find something each day about your foster child to praise.

Be on the lookout constantly for behaviours or actions deserving of praise, but don't be over the top about it. Be sincere and honest in your praise. Wait for unexpected or previously unnoticed good behaviours and praise your foster child for them. And when you see such actions or behaviours, praise immediately, so the child will know exactly what behaviour or action was deemed praiseworthy. It's also very important to look your foster child square in the eye when you praise him or her, and reinforce the positive behaviour, action or trait being praised with a gesture such as a warm smile, a hug, or scruff of the hair while you tell them.

Be exact, and state precisely what action, behaviour or trait you find praiseworthy. And most importantly, never directly follow praise with criticism or negative comments. Let your foster child know what they did right and reward them for it before you let them know what they did wrong and punish them for misbehaving.

So be sure to admire and congratulate your foster child, and celebrate the good person they are growing into by praising their positive actions, behaviours and traits daily. You'll be building a strong sense of self in your foster child and you'll grow closer as a result.

EMOTIONAL WELL-BEING

In your effort to balance very full and hectic lives with your families and your jobs, you may have been neglecting an all-important facet of your foster child's life: their emotional well-being. The first three years of a child's life is a critical time for a child, and the experience of coming into foster care can be very traumatic and destabilizing for them. It's imperative that foster carers, involved adults and social workers make a concerted, joint effort to ensure that a child's emotional needs are met on a daily basis, just as their physical needs are. The effects of not meeting a child's emotional needs, especially during the first three years of life, can have devastating consequences. Violent, disruptive or defiant behaviours can result.

The first three years of life are critical in a number of ways. This is when bonding and emotional separation takes place. If there are interruptions in either of these processes (as there often are when children are placed in foster care), misbehaviours from the child can result.

This can have an effect on their relationships later in life and hinder them in developing their own healthy relationships as adolescents or adults.

During the first three years of life, the brain goes through its most rapid development ever, the likes of which will never be experienced again. By the time they are three years old, a child's brain is already 'hardwired' from the experiences they've had to that point. It's important that these be loving, supportive, safe, positive experiences, so the brain will be conditioned to expect positive things. Unfortunately, a lot of the experiences of fostered children have been frightening, hurtful, abusive, or dangerous, and quite often their brain is conditioned to expect negative occurrences.

Therefore, it's critical that foster carers and other involved adults make a concerted effort to ensure that a foster child's emotional needs are met in a positive, constructive and healthy manner. Social workers should ensure that the child's care providers are stable and consistent, and shouldn't move them around to different foster placements during this important phase (whenever possible). Ensure a foster child feels safe and secure with structured and consistent schedules and routines. Be sure to spend as much quality time with your foster child at this time as possible, regardless of your otherwise busy and hectic lifestyle. A foster child can often sense that such a schedule is stressful to you and it can become a frightening or confusing element for them.

Therefore, it's important to take time out to reassure them that you're never too busy for them. Remember that your foster child's emotional well-being is just as important as their physical well-being, so do your part to ensure your foster child knows he or she is growing up safe, secure, and loved.

YOU CAN'T SPOIL A FOSTER CHILD THROUGH LOVE

Though we all might worry about spoiling our foster child, rest assured that you cannot spoil your foster child with love. Love doesn't spoil children. Love is imperative to a child's healthy development. Foster children need caring adults to spend time with them, play with them, teach them, protect them, and enjoy life with them.

It's a foster carer's job to provide care, safety, and encouragement. The process of growing up provides children with lots of challenges. Try to listen openly and understand their situation, and communicate honestly with them when they have difficulties and letdowns in their life.

Set appropriate limits with your foster child and then adhere to them. Establishing limits with your foster child gives them a sense of safety and security.

Sometimes foster carers do not set limits because they don't want to fight with their foster children. They don't want to cause bad feelings. They may be afraid to ask a child to comply, or they may make a rule and fail to enforce it. They may nag without ever enforcing the rules. None of these behaviours help foster children. When your foster child fails to adhere or comply with the boundaries you've set for them, be firm, yet kind, in your response. This lets them know that you're serious about the rule but dedicated to helping and caring for them. Bear in mind though that each foster child is different and what works for one child may not work for another. For example, one child may respond well to the direct approach of telling them a specific time to be home, where another child may need a gentle reminder that it's now time to come home.

Develop a firm, but kind, manner of making and enforcing your household's rules and expectations. There's no need to fear your foster children, and there should be no need to instill a sense of fear in our foster children in order to get them to comply.

Actively Listening to Your Foster Child

Communicating with your foster children can be a difficult task at times. You may feel like they're not listening to you; they feel like you're not listening to them. Good listening and communication skills are essential to successful foster caring. Your foster child's feelings, views and opinions have worth, and you should make sure you take the time to sit down and listen openly and discuss them honestly.

It seems to be a natural tendency to react rather than to respond. We pass judgment based on our own feelings and experiences. However, responding means being receptive to your foster child's feelings and emotions, and allowing them to express themselves openly and honestly without fear of repercussion from you. By reacting, you send your foster child the message that their feelings and opinions are invalid. But responding and asking questions about why the foster child feels that way opens a dialog that allows them to discuss their feelings further, and allows you a better understanding of where they're coming from.

Responding also gives you an opportunity to work out a solution or a plan of action with your foster child that perhaps they would not have come up with on their own. Your foster child will also appreciate the fact that maybe you do indeed understand how they feel.

It's crucial in these situations to give your foster child your full and undivided attention. Put down your newspaper, stop doing dishes, or turn off the television so you can hear the full situation and make eye contact with your foster child. Keep calm, be inquisitive, and afterwards offer potential solutions to the problem.

Don't discourage your foster child from feeling upset, angry, or frustrated. Our initial instinct may be to say or do something to steer our foster child away from it, but this can be a detrimental tactic. Again, listen to your foster child, ask questions to find out why they are feeling that way, and then offer potential solutions to alleviate the bad feeling.

Just as you do, your foster children have feelings and experience difficult situations. Actively listening and participating with your foster child as they talk about it demonstrates to them that you do care, you want to help and you have similar experiences of your own that they can draw from. Remember, respond - don't react.

CELEBRATE YOUR FOSTER CHILD'S UNIQUENESS

Just like a snowflake or a fingerprint, every child is unique in their own special way. Every child has a unique way of feeling, thinking, and interacting with others. Some children are shy, while others are outgoing; some are active, while others are calm; some are fretful, while others are easy-going. As a loving and nurturing foster carer, it's your job to encourage your foster children to embrace their uniqueness and celebrate their individual qualities.

Allow your foster child to express themselves through their interests. They may find a creative outlet in theatre, dancing or art, or they may be exceptionally talented in the sciences. Encourage them to embrace what they like to do, what interests them, and what makes them happy. Help them realise that they don't need to worry about being 'like everyone else.'

Teach your foster child to make positive choices, and praise them for good deeds, behaviours and positive traits they possess. Encourage them to become actively involved in their community, and introduce them to activities that promote a sense of cooperation and accomplishment. Be firm, yet fair, when handing down discipline for misdeeds or misbehaviours, and make certain the consequences for breaking the rules are clearly defined. Show a cooperative, loving and united front with your partner (if you have one) when it comes to discipline.

Accept and celebrate your foster child's uniqueness. Remember that your foster child is an individual. Allow your foster child to have his or her own personal preferences and feelings, which may be different from your own.

And finally, encourage your foster child to be true to themselves by doing the same. Show your foster child how to make positive choices with the choices you make, and that nobody is perfect and you too make mistakes. Show your foster child that mistakes can be a great learning experience, and that they should not be ashamed or embarrassed about making them.

CONNECT WITH YOUR FOSTER CHILD

We all want to connect and be involved with our foster children. Children of involved foster carers generally feel more confident, assured, and have a higher level of self-esteem. They excel in school and do well in extracurricular activities and with their hobbies.
But is there such a thing as too much involvement? It's imperative when you're becoming involved with your school-aged foster child's activities and education that you recognize the line of what being too involved can be.

Remember, you're becoming involved in your foster child's life. It's important that you don't intrude too much upon it. Children need their space and privacy and they need to be able to develop their own skills, talents and abilities. In your eagerness to help your foster child succeed, it's tempting to step in and start doing things for them because you feel they are doing them incorrectly or inadequately. But remember, you had to learn too, and this is their chance to learn on their own.

Be there to encourage and support your foster child, and offer praise for a job well done. But also remember to step back and allow your foster child to learn from their own mistakes, and to develop their own way of doing things. We all know from our own life experiences that there's always more than just one way to do something, and just because your foster child is doing it differently than you would doesn't make it wrong. Who knows, it could present a terrific opportunity for you to learn from your foster child as well.

In addition, try not to become too overbearing or nosy when it comes to their social life. Be available for them should they need to talk and encourage them to share their troubles with you so you can help them sort through a problem. But if they say they don't want to talk about it or they just need some time to figure things out for themselves, respect that need by letting them know that you're available whenever they need you. This is an important part of growing up, and allowing a foster child to figure his or her own way through things is an integral part of that process.

CHORES!

Chores can help develop a sense of responsibility and self-worth in your foster child. It should be understood by all family members that chores are expected and necessary to a household running successfully and efficiently. They can help create a sense of unity and family and are a great way for your foster child to learn about teamwork. Foster carers should take special care to handle the delegation of chores to foster children so they don't become a source of frustration or create arguments.

Allow your foster child to have an active say in the delegation of chores. Give them choices. We all have household chores that we don't like to do, but if it's a chore the child enjoys doing, then there's less likelihood it will create a battle in the end. Your foster child will most likely appreciate having the chance to be heard and having a choice.

It's imperative that you set parameters early on for the successful completion of a chore. They may not perform up to standard when they first start performing the chore, but show them where improvement is needed and praise them for a strong effort. Also make sure your foster child understands there will be consequences if they only put forth a minimal effort. Ensure that your foster child understands the need for the chore's effective and efficient completion. Set consequences for substandard completion as a team. Make sure they see that if they don't perform their chores, it affects the other members of the team.

Foster carers must work together and be a strong example for their foster children by completing their own chores each day. And don't allow a foster child to undermine your authority by battling with you over a designated chore. Stand your ground and don't give in, and emphasize the consequence and negative effect an uncompleted chore has on the family.

And keep an open mind when a foster child wants to discuss their thoughts or express their opinions about chores. Make sure the conversation stays positive and on target.

CHART YOUR FOSTER CHILD'S ACCOMPLISHMENTS

It can be very frustrating to ask your foster child over and over again to complete their chores without them ever getting done. If this describes your house to a tee, consider designing a chore chart. Chores might include taking out the rubbish, doing the dishes, cleaning their room, or putting laundry in the laundry room.

Each chore has to be done just once or twice a week. Anything more is unrealistic. After your foster child completes each chore, they can put a check mark on the chore chart. At the end of each week, it's very inspiring for both foster carer and child to look at the chore chart and easily see that each designated job was completed. Just like you with your 'to do' lists, your foster child will find great satisfaction in being able to check off each chore as it is completed and take pride knowing they accomplished a set task or list of tasks.

Once you've sat down with your foster child and discussed and designed a chore chart, it's time to discuss the rewards for accomplishing each task listed. Perhaps in your home you decide you will give a set sum for each task accomplished. If you should decide to grant your foster child some sort of monetary allowance, make sure it's age appropriate and granted on a regular basis (and agreed with his/her social worker).

This is a great opportunity for you to teach your foster child the value of both earning and saving money, and also giving back. Perhaps the child can divide their allowance in half: 1/2 to spend and 1/2 to save.

You might also want to consider designing a 'bank book' for each portion of the allowance and tuck each into two separate money jars, and that way you and your foster child will be able to keep track of how much has been saved, how much has been spent.
 If you decide to use non-monetary incentives as chores payment, be sure you set clear parameters for your foster child. Be sure they understand that two hours each weekend of their favourite video game or going to the cinema is only earned by completing the chore list successfully each week. You might want to consider writing these on a slip of paper as 'currency' for the child to keep in their 'privilege bank' and they can cash it in with you when they'd like. Regardless of the method you choose, keep in mind that this can be a valuable tool for both you and your foster child.

HOBBIES ARE HEALTHY

Hobbies benefit foster children in many ways. They give a foster child an opportunity to express themselves, discover themselves, and build self-esteem. They are also great educational tools. A foster child interested in rock collecting learns about geology and science, and a child, in writing stories learns about sentence structure and proper grammar.

Hobbies teach foster children to set and achieve goals, solve problems, and make decisions. They can also set the course for what your foster child becomes later in life, as they often turn into lifelong interests or careers.

Foster children who have hobbies are usually following in their carers footsteps, so set a good example by pursuing your own hobby. Your foster child will need space for their hobby, so find an area designated specifically for the hobby so they can work on it. Realise that hobbies can sometimes be quite messy, so be ready for the mess, as it comes with the territory.

Be available to your foster child to provide guidance, support, and encouragement. This is a great time to teach your foster child strong work habits, such as following directions closely, setting goals, and proper planning and organization. Show them that nothing worthwhile is ever easy, especially when they begin to become frustrated with their progress. It's also a good time to teach them about personal responsibility and show them how important it is to properly care for their work area and their 'tools of the trade.'

Children will be more encouraged to work on their hobbies if activities like watching television or playing video games are limited. It's been noted by experts that by age 15, the average child has spent more time watching television than sitting in a classroom. Again, here's where setting a good example is crucial. Instead of watching that four-hour football game or those Soaps on Saturday, turn the TV off and work on your own hobby. Your foster child may want to join in or work on his or her own, as a result.

Hobbies are rewarding and enriching parts of our lives, so encourage your foster child to explore their own interests and find a hobby of their very own.

CHAPTER 3
THE DAY TO DAY...

EATING TOGETHER

Recent studies have shown that not only do children like to sit down at the dinner table and eat a meal with their carers, but they also are more likely to eat a well-balanced, nutritious meal when they do. But with the hectic lives we seem to lead these days, getting the family all together in the same place at the same time can be a difficult chore. Between work schedules, after-school activities, errands, and the like, it seems we have less and less time. But with a few simple ideas and some planning, meal time can be an enjoyable and treasured time.

Designate no less than one night per week to have a sit-down meal with your family. Sunday nights are usually a good choice for this, because you have more time to relax and the weekend chores have been completed.

Involve your foster children in the meal planning and preparation. This gives them a strong sense of self and the foundation for a lifetime of healthy meal planning and preparation.

Make sure the television is off and make it a rule that all phone calls go to voice mail or the answering machine during the meal. Take this time to talk to one another and enjoy one another's company. This is a great time to reconnect and find out what events happened this week. Take your time eating, and teach your foster children how to do the same in the process. Eating slowly is a healthy habit. Don't jump up and start clearing dishes and putting things away until everyone is done eating and talking.

On those days that you can't sit down as a family, try to make a habit of sitting down and chatting with your foster child while they are eating, instead of rushing around catching up on the chores. This shows them that you're interested, and that you care and want to be an involved and important part of their everyday life.

REGULAR ROUTINES

Regular schedules provide the day with a structure that orders a young child's world. Although predictability can be tiresome for adults, children thrive on repetition and routine. Schedules begin from the first days of life. Babies, especially, need regular sleep and meal programs and even routines leading up to those activities.

As they get older, when a child knows what is going to happen and who is going to be there, it allows them to think and feel more independently, and feel more safe and secure. A disrupted routine can set a child off and cause them to feel insecure and irritable.
Dinner time is a great place to start setting a routine. Sitting together at the dinner table gives children the opportunity to share their day and talk about their feelings. This is also a great time to include some responsibility in your child's routine, such as helping to set or clear the table.

And regardless of how exhausted you or your foster children may be, don't be tempted to skip winding down from the day. This is part of a night time ritual and allows both foster child and carer to decompress after a busy day. It also helps bedtime go more smoothly. This is usually the time of day when foster carer and child can spend some quality time together, so fight the urge to start the laundry or do the dishes until after your foster child has gone to bed. If this isn't possible, consider trading off these duties with your partner each night to ensure your foster child has quality time with each carer on a regular basis. Take the time to find out what wind-down strategy works best for your foster child. Some children are actually energized instead of relaxed by a warm bath, so if that's the case with your foster child, bath time should be saved for a different time of day. Whatever routine you settle on, make it quiet, relaxing, and tranquil for everyone.

And though routines are essential, there should be some room to be flexible as well. You might be out late at night on a family outing, or have unexpected company show up that may result in a skipped meal or a nap in the car while running errands in the evening. In these instances, it's important for you to keep your cool. If you express frustration or anger about the disruption of the routine, your foster child will as well. Prepare children for such unexpected events and show them that though it can happen from time to time, the routine will return the next day.

THE POSITIVE INFLUENCE OF EDUCATION

It has been shown many times over in research studies that a carer who is involved in their foster child's education has a positive impact. It's reflected in improved grades and test scores, strong attendance, a higher rate of homework completion, higher graduation rates, improved attitudes and behaviours in the foster child, as well as the child being more likely to become involved in positive extra-curricular activities. Send out the message early in your foster child's education that your home is an involved and active supporter of their learning.

Probably the most important element of a positive learning environment at home is structure. But what is too little or too much? If you're too lenient or expect too little, your child may become disorganized or unmotivated. If you're too rigid and strict, it can cause undue pressure or cause your child to feel unable to deliver on your expectations.

So what's the best way to meet in the middle and create a positive learning environment for your foster child at home?

Help your foster child develop a work area where they can study and focus without being interrupted. Children usually do better when they have a private study area away from interruption. If your foster child prefers doing their work at the kitchen table, make sure other family members understand that the kitchen is off-limits during study time. Make sure your foster child has plenty of supplies and reference materials available and that the area has plenty of light. Regardless of its location, ensure the area is quiet and that your foster child can study and work uninterrupted.

Agree on a regular time for studying. To help your foster child make homework a habit, schedule a set time each day for homework. Perhaps breaking study time up into smaller increments would work better for your foster child than one solid period. Work with your foster child to find out what works best for them. In addition, be sure your foster child has a sufficient break between the time they arrive home from school and the time they sit down to work, in order to 'decompress' from their school day.

Help your foster child develop a method of keeping track of homework assignments. This can be a difficult chore for some students. Developing a successful way of keeping track of assignments, then scratching them off as completed, helps them develop a productive method for accomplishing tasks later in life.

Develop a positive line of communication with your foster child's teacher. Teachers are usually very willing and excited to work with an involved foster carer to help the child's overall success in school. Whether it's notes sent back and forth in your foster child's backpack or an e-mail exchange, make sure the teacher knows you are open for suggestions as to how to better assist them in the homework and study process at home.

THE TRUTH ABOUT LYING

Honesty and dishonesty are learned in the home. Foster carers are often concerned when their foster child or adolescent lies.

Young children often make up stories and tell tall tales. This is normal, because they enjoy hearing stories and making up stories for fun. These young children may blur the distinction between reality and fantasy. This is probably more a result of an active imagination than an attempt to deliberately lie about something.

An older child or adolescent may tell a lie to be self-serving, such as denying responsibility or to try to get out of a chore or task. Carers should respond to isolated instances of lying by talking with the youngster about the importance of truthfulness, honesty and trust.

Some adolescents discover that lying may be considered acceptable in certain situations, such as not telling a boyfriend or girlfriend the real reasons for breaking up with them because they don't want to hurt their feelings. Other adolescents may lie to protect their privacy or to help them feel psychologically separate and independent from their carers.

Carers are the most important role models for their foster children. When a foster child or adolescent lies, carers should take some time to have a serious talk and discuss the difference between make believe and reality, and lying and telling the truth. They should open an honest line of communication to find out exactly why the foster child chose to tell a lie, and to discuss alternatives to lying. A carer should lead by example and never lie, and when they are caught in a lie, express remorse and regret for making a conscious decision to tell a lie. Clear, understandable consequences for lying should be discussed with the foster child early on.

However, some forms of lying are a cause for concern, and might indicate an underlying emotional problem. Some foster children who know the difference between truthfulness and lying tell elaborate stories which appear believable. Children or adolescents usually relate these stories with enthusiasm because they receive a lot of attention as they tell the lie.

Other children or adolescents who otherwise seem responsible fall into a pattern of repetitive lying. They often feel that lying is the easiest way to deal with the demands of carers, teachers and friends. These children are usually not trying to be bad or malicious, but the repetitive pattern of lying becomes a bad habit. A serious repetitive pattern of lying should be cause for concern. Talk to the child's social worker to find out whether professional help is needed.

THE WHYS OF WHINING

"WAAAAAAAAAAAH!"
It's irritating, it's frustrating and it gets on your last nerve. Though it's obnoxious and unacceptable, it's actually an effective way for your foster child to get your attention. It's whining. But, like other bad habits, you can nip it in the bud early on with a few simple strategies to teach your foster child that there are other appropriate, effective forms of communicating with you.

First, try limiting the situations that trigger it. Avoid extra errands when the foster children are hungry. Don't let them get involved in a frustrating game or project prior to bedtime. Pay attention when your foster child is talking, as sometimes whining is a reaction when a child feels you aren't giving them your full attention. Praise them for not whining and talking in a normal and understandable voice that allows you to fully understand what they are saying to you.

When the whining begins, don't overreact. Keep your response simple, calm and neutral. Ask your foster child to repeat the request in a normal tone. When giving in seems inevitable, don't delay. If you must finish the shopping so that you can put dinner on the table, for instance, and your foster child starts whining for a snack, offer something healthy right away.

If you have an older child that's developing a whining habit, suggest they come up with a solution to their perceived boredom or other voiced problem. If you suggest possible alternatives, it might just prolong the child's whining.

Sometimes whining can be the result of trauma and trouble in their life or school may be at the root. Additional positive attention and quality one-on-one time may be just the medicine your foster child needs at a time like this. Your Fostering Support Worker can also suggest alternatives to curb whining should the positive attention and disciplinary actions be ineffective.

TRAINING THE FUSSY EATER

Toddlers can be fussy eaters who may refuse to try a new food at least half of the time. Approximately half of all toddlers fit this description, so it is no wonder that food issues are a source of stress for foster carers.

Establishing healthy eating patterns is important to avoid problems such as obesity and eating disorders later in life. Various strategies can help your foster child accept a wider range of foods. It may be necessary to offer a food to your foster child as many as 10 different times before they choose to eat it. The problem is, many carers get frustrated and give up before the fourth or fifth try.

Try to make foods fun. Colourful foods like carrot sticks, raisins, apples, grapes, cheese sticks and crackers can all be fun and healthy choices for your growing foster child. Explain to them that eating good food is important so they'll grow big and strong, and how it will help them to run faster and play longer.

Foster children learn behaviours from their foster carers. If you restrict yourself to a narrow range of foods, your foster child will take notice and mimic your caution. Don't limit your foster child's food variety to only those foods you prefer. It may be that your foster child's tastes are different from yours, and perhaps you are simply serving them foods they don't happen to like. Try to set a good example and try a variety of foods in front of your foster child. It could motivate them to do the same.

If your foster child seems healthy and energetic, then they are eating enough. If you are still concerned, keep an eye on how much food they actually eat over the course of a day. Children tend to graze constantly, rather than restrict their eating to three meals per day like adults. You may be surprised how those little handfuls and snacks add up. For further reassurance, check your foster child's growth and weight charts, or check with your foster child's social worker.

Try not to worry and remember that unless a child is ill, they will eat. Children are very good at judging their hunger and fullness signals. Try to stay relaxed about mealtimes and offer your foster child a wide variety of foods, and most importantly, remember to set a good example by trying a wide variety of foods yourself. You may discover you and your foster child share a new found favourite food!

TEACH YOUR FOSTER CHILD RESPECT

One of the most important things you can teach your foster child is respect, and the best way to teach respect is to show respect. When a child experiences respect, they know what it feels like and they begin to understand how important it is.

Keep in mind the saying, "Do unto others as you would have them do unto you."
Respect is an attitude. Being respectful helps a foster child succeed in life. If children don't have respect for peers, authority, or themselves, it's almost impossible for them to succeed. A respectful child takes care of belongings and responsibilities, and a respectful child gets along with peers.

Schools teach children about respect, but foster carers have the most influence on how respectful foster children become. Until foster children show respect at home, it's unlikely they will show it anywhere else.

How can you show respect to your foster child? If you do something wrong, admit it and apologize. Don't embarrass, insult or make fun of your foster child. Compliment them and let your foster child make choices and take responsibility. Listen to your foster child's side of the story before making a decision on an issue or problem. Be polite and use "please" and "thank you" when asking them to do things. Knock before entering your foster child's room. Keep promises. Show your foster child that you mean what you say. And give your foster child your full attention.

And most importantly, teach your foster children that respect is earned. Make sure that you are leading by example and modelling respectful behaviour. Be a law-abiding citizen. Show concern for your environment, animals and other people. Openly and honestly discuss examples of witnessed disrespect.

In addition, teach your foster child to respect themselves. Self-respect is one of the most important forms of respect. Once we respect ourselves, it is easier to respect others.
Help them set and achieve goals. Encourage honesty and teach them that people make mistakes, and that they are the best way to learn.

Most importantly, praise your foster child often for good deeds, behaviours or traits, and tell them you care about them at least several times each day. You're sure to raise a child capable of giving and gaining respect.

Foster carers also play an essential role in teaching foster children how to form healthy relationships and grow into socially adept individuals. This social competence allows foster children to be cooperative and generous, express their feelings, and empathize with others.

The most effective way to teach foster children this lesson is by modelling the behaviour you want to encourage. Every time you say "please" or lend a helping hand, you are showing your foster children how you would like them to act. Ask for your children's help with daily tasks, and accept their offers of help. Praise your foster child's good behaviour often, and help them to realise how good it feels inside to do a good deed or be generous with another person.

Socially competent children are ones who have a strong sense of self-worth and importance. When a child feels good about themselves, it's easy for them to treat others in a positive, helpful manner.

Encourage acts of generosity through sharing and cooperation. Let your foster child know when it's someone else's turn with a toy or on the swing and praise their ability to recognize this on their own. Thank them for being polite and respectful and for sharing and cooperating.

Children know from their own experiences that words can hurt, and that name-calling, teasing, or excluding others affects how people feel. Children want to be treated fairly, but they don't always understand how to treat others the same way. One way to teach fairness is to explain a rule to your foster child, pointing out that it applies to him or her as well as to others.

TWO-WAY COMMUNICATION

One of the most frustrating challenges you face as a foster carer is communicating effectively with your foster child. Though you may strive to open an honest two-way line of communication with your foster child, it can be frustrating when it appears as though their attention isn't solely on you or the conversation at hand. Yet you may find it's perfectly acceptable to discuss things with them while reading the paper, folding clothes, or working on the computer, and then are often left wondering when the lines of communication broke.

Children are by nature easily distracted and not always responsive to their environment. It is the responsibility of the foster carer to emphasize positive patterns of communication and ensure that the foster child learns that ignoring communication is not acceptable. Early prevention, in the form of educating your foster child about the proper forms of communication, is the key to ensuring that the non-verbal agreement does not take hold. Teach your foster child by example. Remain completely and totally focused on them and the conversation at hand. Turn off the television, allow calls to go to the voicemail, or go into a room where there are no distractions.

Talk to your foster child, and explain to them in age-appropriate terms how they are communicating and why their method doesn't work. Show your foster child how to communicate effectively, even when the questions are hard.

Make yourself an active listener. Let them voice their opinion or side of the story and ask questions to ensure you understand their viewpoint.

Be consistent in the manner in which you communicate with you foster child. Send the same message with each and every interaction. Allow your foster child to see that you will call their attention to those times that the unwanted behaviour rears its ugly head.

Children will be children, and they will sometimes be distracted and non-communicative. You are the expert in knowing your foster child's behaviour and can best judge the improvement in their communications. The best way to ensure healthy communication patterns is to model positive communication skills.

Do As I Say and As I Do

Children learn to imitate at a very young age. It's how they learn to behave, care for themselves, develop new skills, and communicate with others. From their earliest moments they watch their carers closely and pattern their own behaviour and beliefs on what they see. Your examples will become permanent images, which will shape their attitudes and actions for the rest of their life.

It's important to be responsible, consistent and caring with your foster child. This also holds true for the relationship you have with your partner and other family members and friends that are also a part of your foster child's life. Own up to mistakes when you make them, and communicate openly and honestly with all family members.

It's also important to take good care of yourself. When you're focusing on what's best for your foster child, it's easy to neglect your own needs. Your foster child and your family are counting on you physically and emotionally, so it's imperative that you teach your foster child by example that taking care of yourself helps you to take care of them and the rest of your family. This shows your foster child that not only do you care for them and the rest of the family, but you care for yourself as well. This is an important step in teaching your foster child about self-esteem. It may involve getting a babysitter and treating yourself to dinner and the cinema, or doing another favourite activity on your own (or with your partner!). This teaches your foster child that you are not only their foster carer, but your own person with your own interests and needs, and also gives them a chance to show you how well they can do without you with them for a while.

It's also important to nurture your relationship with your partner. Let your foster child see that you communicate in a positive and healthy manner with one another, and show love and affection for one another, so that your foster child can begin to learn early on what a healthy relationship should be like.

You'll soon see your foster child patterning many of his or her behaviours after your own. So make sure that what you say and do around your foster child will help to build a strong sense of security and self-esteem.

Encouraging Play

We've all heard the phrase, "Oh, that's child's play." It implies that something is easy, frivolous and unimportant in the overall scheme of things. But to a child, child's play is essential to their mental, social, emotional, and physical development.

We all know that children like to play. But what we may not know is the importance of play in a child's life. Play is essential to every area of a child's growth and development.

Play provides a means for energy to be put to use. It strengthens and refines small and large motor skills, and it builds stamina and strength. Sensory learning develops mostly through play. Play is significant to physical development in that without it, the body could not grow and develop normally.

Children possess a natural curiosity. They explore, learn, and make sense out of their environment by playing. Foster carers can support this learning activity by ensuring age appropriate toys, materials and environments are available to the child.

Play enables children to know things about the world and to discover information essential to learning. Through play, children learn basic concepts such as colours, counting, how to build things, and how to solve problems. Thinking and reasoning skills are at work every time a child engages in some type of play.

Children learn to relate to one another, negotiate roles, share, and obey rules through play. They also learn how to belong to a group and how to be part of a team. A child obtains and retains friends through play.

Play fulfills many needs including a sense of accomplishment, successfully giving and receiving attention, and the need for self-esteem. It helps them to develop a strong sense of self, and is emotionally satisfying to them. They learn about fairness, and through pretending, learn appropriate ways of expressing emotion such as anger, fear, frustration, and stress, and discover ways of dealing with these feelings.

So encourage your foster child's play. Colour pictures, make finger paintings, build buildings and imaginary cities with blocks, and build a tent in the middle of the living room to go camping! And as we all know, childhood is fleeting, so let them enjoy being a kid while they are one.

EXPECT THE BEST

Expect the best from your foster child. If you expect the best behaviour and performance from your foster child, it's often what you will get. Children pick up on our beliefs about them, form a self-concept that matches that belief, and perform accordingly. If we expect them to be lazy, they'll be lazy, which will confirm our expectations for them, and the cycle toward failure is started. If, on the other hand, you expect your foster children to be successful, productive, creative, and responsible, and honestly believe it to be true, then your foster child can't help but rise to the occasion and confirm your best opinions of them with their positive actions. So expect nothing but the best from your foster child and watch them fulfill your expectations.

Praise your foster child often when they perform a good deed or accomplish a new task. Set simple, clear and consistent rules so your foster child knows exactly what is expected and the consequences of misbehaving or breaking the rules. Maintain a consistent daily routine for your foster child as much as possible, and make sure your foster child gets lots of physical activity and time to play and socialize with their friends. Encourage your foster child to learn how to make appropriate choices, and encourage your foster child to do things for themselves. Allow your foster child to talk about strong feelings, which will help them work through their anger and frustration.

Above all, be a positive role model for your foster child, as their strongest educator is your example. Take care of yourself, and expect the best from yourself. Make appropriate choices and be firm, yet fair, when disciplining your foster child. Make sure to spend lots of quality time with your foster child, and encourage them to become involved in activities that foster cooperation and a sense of accomplishment. If you have great expectations of your foster child, you'll be greatly pleased in the end.

GET INVOLVED

It's probably no secret that children who have involved carers are happier, healthy, and well-adjusted, and excel at their educational and extra-curricular pursuits. It can increase their cognitive development, keep them motivated, strengthen the foster carer-child relationship, and have a direct positive influence on their overall academic achievement. In turn, it can also help foster carers to achieve a positive outlook on their parenting, increase their own self confidence and self-esteem, and most likely feel more satisfied with their foster child's educational experience at school.

But where do you get involved? With today's busy schedules between home, work, and school, it may feel like the average foster family has very little quality time to offer. However, different options and levels of commitment are available to fit every foster carers's availability, and with some careful planning and dedication, you can make it a positive experience for both yourself and your foster child.

First of all, discover what your foster child is most passionate about. Maybe you've thought about volunteering for the school cake sale to raise money, but your foster child is actually more actively involved in local groups. If that's the case, then maybe get together with other foster carers and see what you can organize that may be of interest to your foster child and theirs.

It's also important to consider what skills, talents and abilities you can bring to the table. Maybe your foster child's school is in desperate need of your help organizing a fundraiser, but your skills in sewing and designing might better serve the school if you were to help make the costumes for the school play.

Remember, you want this to be a positive experience for both of you, and if your child senses that you're not happy with what you've chosen to become involved in, then they likely will not be happy either.

But the bottom line is to get involved and stay involved. Children of involved foster carers are less likely to get into mischief, have emotional problems, or have trouble in school. You benefit by connecting with and staying connected to your foster child. It's a win-win situation for you both.

LEARN FROM YOUR MISTAKES

Everyone makes mistakes. Granted, some mistakes are more significant than others and harder to get over, but they are a part of life. How individuals deal with those mistakes is significant to their self-esteem. Remember, we can't always control what happens, but we can control how we respond!

Children who are taught from an early age to admit to their mistakes understand that it's not a crime to make one, and they seem to have the ability to cope much better with them. They recognize that a mistake was made and admit the error. Most importantly, these children also develop a strategy to change the mistake and not do the same thing again.

The process of making and learning from mistakes is an extremely valuable life skill for everyone, because learning involves risks. Children don't succeed every time they take a risk, but they try something new and most likely learn from it as a result.

Children with low self-esteem deal with making a mistake quite differently. More often than not, these children use the experience to devalue themselves. Instead of looking at the error as an opportunity to learn, these children interpret the experience as a reason to quit and never try again. They view it as a devaluing and humiliating experience.

You can help your foster child to cope with mistakes by first making sure they understand that everyone makes mistakes, even you. Own up to your own mistakes to teach them there's no shame in making them. Make sure they understand that it's okay to make mistakes. This presents a great opportunity to tell your foster child what you've learned to do differently the next time. Then, offer strategies to turn mistakes into learning opportunities. In the process, you can provide your foster child with an opportunity to enhance their self-esteem and accept responsibility for the mistakes they make. Help your foster child to realise that the mistake is the problem, and not them. Then help them develop a positive plan for the next time around, and what they'll do differently the next time to avoid making the same mistake again.

MAKE QUALITY TIME COUNT

In today's busy world, work, household chores and social activities all put a strain on your time with your foster child. But as you well know (and we discussed in an earlier chapter), it's imperative that you spend quality time together. It helps strengthen the bond between foster carer and foster child, and lets your foster child know you can be trusted and counted on. Children who spend quality time with their carers often do better in school, and excel in extracurricular activities, hobbies or sports. And though it can be 'scheduled' to a degree, it's something that happens when you least expect it.

Therefore, it's important that you do spend as much time as possible with your foster child in a relaxed atmosphere and do things together that you both enjoy.

But you're asking yourself, "Where am I going to find the time? My schedule's crazy enough as it is!" Well, for something as important as your foster child, you need to start digging around in that crazy schedule and find the time.

Prioritizing is the key. Here are some helpful suggestions on how to make the most of your time and find quality time where you least expect it:

Look at your household chore list and decide which ones can be left undone or be done imperfectly in order to make more family time. You might also want to consider leaving certain things until after your foster child has gone to bed to make the most of your time together.

Make some of your everyday routines together count. Sing some favourite silly songs on the way to daycare, or use that drive to and from school as a great opportunity to discuss what's happening in your foster child's life.

If you have more than one foster child, realise that each of them needs your individual attention. You may really have to juggle things around to make this happen, but try to be flexible and creative when spending time with each of your foster children (and your own children). And no matter what, don't skip those individual times with each child. When you do that, you show them they're lower down on the priority list than the dry cleaning or the shopping.

Children thrive on stability and routines, so plan your quality times so that they can take place regularly. Maybe you can walk the dog together on weekend mornings, take a shopping trip together, have a scheduled night each week for a sit-down dinner together, or take a trip to the park.

Verbal Abuse and How to Stop the Cycle

"Sticks and stones may break my bones, but names will never hurt me."

That's just not true. Name-calling hurts— especially when the person doing it is a parent, a teacher, or a foster carer. Yelling and screaming might have been the way you were brought up, and you might think it worked for you, so why wouldn't it work for your foster children? But did it? Remember how it made you feel. You probably felt belittled, devalued, and insignificant. You certainly don't want your foster children to feel that way. It may cause emotional trauma that can result in long-term hurt. Among other things, verbal abuse can undermine your foster child's self-esteem, damage his or her ability to trust and form relationships, and chip away at his or her academic and social skills. Name-calling, swearing, insulting, threatening bodily harm, blaming or using sarcasm are all forms of verbal abuse.

What are the signs that a child is suffering (or may have suffered) from verbal abuse? They may have a very negative self-image. They may commit acts that are self-destructive, such as cutting, hitting or scratching themselves, as well as other reckless and dangerous activities. They may exhibit physical aggression, be delinquent in school, or display interpersonal problems. They may hit other children, frequently fight with classmates at school, or be cruel to animals. They may also exhibit delays in their social, physical, academic or emotional development.

Recent research suggests that children who suffer from verbal abuse are highly likely to become victims of abuse later in life, become abusive themselves, or become depressed and self-destructive later in life

It's normal for most foster carers, at one time or another, to feel frustrated and angry with their foster children. You must not lash out verbally in these instances and say things they you will later regret. It's when these feelings become more and more frequent that there is cause for concern. If this describes you, it's imperative that you seek professional help to learn more positive, meaningful and constructive forms of discipline, and for help in learning methods to control your anger. Remember to give yourself a time out if you feel an outburst coming on. Do not say mean, sarcastic or belittling things to your foster child.

Remember, your child learns what he or she lives. Don't be a bad example and teach him or her bad behaviour early on.

Also remember that your foster child is a precious gift and should be treated with kindness, respect and tenderness. If you exhibit these to your foster child on a daily basis, they will learn what they live and grow to do the same as adults.

Control Your Anger ....Don't Let It Control You

Anger can be a paralyzing and debilitating condition. But it can be a terrifying and degrading experience for your foster child if you're taking your anger out on them. Physical and verbal abuse of a child can have lasting and lethal implications, so it's crucial that as a foster carer, you do whatever is necessary to keep your anger in check.

As a foster carer, you have a wonderful opportunity to undo the wrongs that may have been done to you as a child, if you had an angry and abusive parent or carer. Perhaps your past is filled with unresolved hurt and anger. If so, take the necessary steps to heal yourself. If you don't, you could unwillingly and unthinkingly harm your foster child. Studies have shown that children whose foster carers often expresses anger are more likely to be difficult to discipline. Identify problems from your past and honestly look at current situations that are angering you. Maybe you aren't fulfilled at work; perhaps you and your partner are having relationship troubles, or maybe you have other personal issues or unfulfilled goals that are bothering you. If all your foster child ever sees is your angry face and hears an angry voice, that's what they'll most likely grow into as well. If you recognize yourself here please speak to your Fostering Support Worker to get some help.

It's important to 'pick your battles' when caring for foster children. Accidents and nuisances don't warrant the energy and agony it takes to get angry. But misbehaviours such as a child hurting themselves, others or property demand a firm, quick and appropriate response from you.

You will probably have to continually remind yourself that the small stuff isn't worth getting worked up over. And remind yourself also that you're the one in control of your anger; don't let your anger control you. Put yourself in time out, take a deep breath, walk away, and do whatever you have to in order to get a grip on yourself before addressing the situation, if you feel your anger coming on strong.

CHAPTER 4.

EFFECTIVE DISCIPLINE

Disciplining a child is one of the most important, yet difficult, roles of being a foster carer. Effective discipline teaches a child to be self-disciplined later in life. It helps your foster child grow up to be happy and well-adjusted. Effective and positive discipline teaches and guides children, and helps them to feel safe, secure, and valued.

Discipline should be based on a child's age, development and temperament. A foster carer's goals by disciplining their foster child is to protect them from danger, to help them learn self-control and self-discipline and to develop a sense of responsibility. Children should be respectful of their carers' authority. If they're disciplined harshly or unfairly, especially if punishment includes shouting or humiliating, it will make it difficult, if not impossible, for a child to respect and trust their carer.

Foster carers must be consistent in their discipline. Discipline that's not consistent is confusing to children, no matter how old they are. If foster carers are inconsistent in the way they discipline their foster children, the foster children may find it hard to respect them. It can also indirectly encourage misbehaving and result in confusion and frustration for the child. Discipline must also be fair. Foster carers must make sure that the punishment fits the crime, and is neither too severe nor too lax. The consequences of their actions should be related to their behaviour. You should discuss this with the child's social worker and your fostering support worker.

In order to discourage bad behaviour, give your foster child choices about what to do. He or she will appreciate the chance to make decisions. Make sure rules that protect the safety, health and well-being of your foster child are given top priority. If your foster child is irritable, tired or upset, be understanding and try to help calm them down. It's important to keep in mind that bad behaviour can sometimes be circumstantial.
Encourage positive behaviour in your foster child by spending quality time alone with them each day. Give your foster child hugs, cuddles or a gentle pat on the back, and give praise when praise is due. If your foster child is angry or sad, try to understand why. Teach your foster child good behaviour by setting a good example and behaving properly and appropriately yourself.

CRYSTAL CLEAR RULES

The world is a far more scary and complicated place than it was when you were a child (or so it seems!). As a result, it's imperative that you set adequate, yet fair boundaries with your foster child. It's a very important role in your foster caring responsibilities.

Children must make difficult decisions each day, and if they don't have clear, firm boundaries set, they may not always make the wisest choices. Limits teach children proper restraint in social and individual activities and provide children with necessary structure and security to assist in healthy development. Setting limits also provides children with guidance before they have an opportunity to get into trouble, thus making them more successful with everyday life.

A foster child's age and developmental level needs to be considered when setting limits. All children have a need for independence and individualization;

However, they also need structure, security and foster carer involvement. It goes without saying that the needs of a 2-year-old vary greatly from those of a teenager. A toddler has a strong desire to explore and investigate, but parameters need to be set to ensure their safety while doing so. Teenagers need to be able to be individual and independent, but with strong guidance and influence, they are more likely to make smart choices in difficult situations.

Limits should be discussed and set prior to a situation. Though situations arise that weren't planned on, daily situations should have set limits and expectations. A teenager who breaks curfew may have the privilege of going out with friends revoked until they learn respect for the rules. A foster child who misbehaves while playing with a friend may need to be separated from the fun until they can learn to properly behave.
Children respond in a positive manner in an environment in which they know what to expect and what is expected of them. A foster child will be more respectful towards rules and more willing to abide by them if the rules are clear and consistent. Additionally, it's crucial that once a limit is set that you stick to it. A child is less likely to try to manipulate a caregiver into changing the limits when their experience has been that there's no bending on the limits. And remember, you are the one who sets the limits and lays down the law. There's no need to argue with your foster child. Be firm and consistent, and they will be less likely to challenge the rules and will accept the consequences.

Handling Conflict at Home

Some foster carers may worry that setting strict rules may distance them from their foster children. But this simply isn't the case. Though they may gripe and complain and get upset when you become the enforcer, they realise deep down that this shows you care. These parameters you set and enforce make your foster child feel loved, safe, and secure.
It's never easy developing and introducing rules. Foster carers may tend to avoid setting rules because they fear confrontation and unpleasantness, but the uncomfortable stuff isn't necessarily a reflection on your relationship with your foster child, it's just the nature of childhood - breaking rules and pushing limits is a part of growing up. You may tend to want to beg your foster child sometimes, but when you're laying down the law, that just isn't possible. Your primary role is to protect, nurture and provide for your foster child.

When foster children break rules, carers often overreact with harsh, disproportionate, and unenforceable punishments, which undermines the effectiveness of setting rules. Instead, when you first tell your foster child about a new rule, discuss the consequences of breaking that rule - what the punishment will be and how it will be carried out. Consequences must go hand in hand with limits so that your foster child knows what the cost of breaking the rules will be. The punishments you set should be reasonable and related to the violation. For example, if you catch your foster child and his/her friends smoking, you might "ground" him/her by restricting his/her social activities for two weeks.

Punishments should only involve the penalties you discussed before the rule was broken. Also, never issue empty threats. It's understandable that you'll be angry when house rules are broken, and sharing your feelings of anger, disappointment, or sadness can have a powerfully motivating effect on your child. Since we're all more inclined to say things we don't mean when we're upset, it's sometimes best to give ourselves a time-out period to cool off before we say something we don't mean.

Make the ground rules crystal clear to your foster child. It's imperative that you are consistent and follow through with a defined disciplinary action after each breach of the rules, and that your foster child understands the reasons why. Don't forget to discuss sanctions and penalties with your support worker and the child's social worker.

CLEAR EXPECTATIONS

Sometimes it can be very challenging to communicate anything with your foster child. Setting clear expectations regarding what is acceptable behaviour and what is not is imperative to successfully teaching your foster child right from wrong. If the parameters are muddled or the child learns that in one situation the rules hold true, yet in another situation the same rule does not, it makes for confusion and frustration on both sides.

Sit down with your foster child well in advance and outline the expectations and consequences of misbehaving. Make it clear that under no circumstances is there any room for negotiation at the time of the breach, and that should such a behaviour occur, you intend to be firm in your discipline. Rules regarding your foster child's safety, health or well-being should have no room for negotiation when being set or enforced. Other rules

92

can be openly and honestly discussed with your foster child and an action should be agreed that both carer and child can agree upon. If necessary, make a contract between yourself and your foster child. Lay it all out in black and white, in language your foster child can clearly understand. For younger children, you might want to develop a good behaviour chart within the contract, and for each week that goes by without any breaches being noted, a favourite or special activity might be earned. The connection between good deeds and special time with carers might be just the currency they understand.

All foster children need to understand that disciplining them is your way of teaching them what is acceptable behaviour and what isn't. It may seem as though children fight rules and boundaries, but they really do know that such parameters are meant for their well-being, health, and safety, and that they will enable them to grow into mature individuals capable of making wise decisions.

"Because" Just Isn't the Answer

Children are inquisitive by nature. When they are younger, it's usually because they want to better understand something. When they are older, it's because they want to better understand why you think something is important and why they should feel the same way. Regardless of their age, it's imperative that your foster child understands that there is no room for questioning the rules and expectations you set and the consequences of breaking the rules.

Younger children usually do not understand a lengthy explanation of why it's important that they be home from their friend's home at a certain time or why they aren't allowed to play ball in the house. But the one thing they do strive to do most of the time is to make their foster carers proud and happy. So when a young child asks "Why?" or "Why not?" when they are told they can't play with something or someone or why they have to obey a rule you've set, simply explain to them, "because it makes me happy when you follow the house rules and do what I have asked of you." You should avoid using the term, "Because I said so," as that only adds to the child's frustration and confusion.

Older children, adolescents and teenagers alike will probably require more from your explanation. When they question "Why?" or "Why not?" it's best to directly, honestly and clearly state your reasoning. Eg. "I asked you to be home by 10 p.m. because we have to be at the dentist's office first thing in the morning for your check-up and we can't be late." It is also a great opportunity for you to reiterate the consequences of breaking the rule. "If you are not home by 10 p.m., you'll be grounded from going to your friend's house for a week." Be consistent, be firm, and be clear.

Though your foster child may challenge you by asking your reasoning for a rule that has been put in place, they are also showing their growth as an individual thinker. So try not to get angry or frustrated when they do so; realise it's their way of understanding the world around them.

CONSISTENCY IS KEY

Consistency is key to successfully teaching your foster child right from wrong when disciplining them. It keeps small episodes of poor behaviour from later becoming bigger and worse episodes of behaviour. You have to stand firm and mean it when you say, "Turn off the television now" or "No dessert after dinner because you didn't touch your food."

Consistency teaches your foster child that there are defined consequences for poor behaviour and inappropriate or unacceptable actions. Inconsistency when disciplining makes you directly responsible for your foster child's misbehaviour and doesn't teach them how to be responsible for their actions.

It's also important that each carer be consistent with the discipline. If one carer is too strict and the other is too lenient, the foster child will latch on to that and try to manipulate the situation to his or her advantage. Carers must agree on disciplinary action in advance and make a commitment to one another to be consistent in implementing and following through with the consequences. It's imperative that you parent on common ground. Openly and honestly discuss these parameters with your partner and your foster child in advance, so that if discipline is needed, the consequences of poor behaviour are well understood in advance. Any disagreements between carers should be discussed out of the child's earshot.

Consistency is about being strong and standing firm, even when doing so is extremely difficult or exhausting. It can sometimes be hard to come home after a hard day at work only to find a hard night of caring in front of you. Your foster child will consistently test the boundaries and 'push the envelope' with you to see if there's any play in those consequences. By standing firm, you are showing there is not, and that you expect them to do nothing less than take responsibility for their actions.

Follow-Through

Let's face it. There are some days when it would just be easier to let your foster child have his or her own way rather than feeling like you're fighting a losing battle when trying to discipline them. They beg, plead, cry, barter and scream - anything to get out of doing the time for their "crime". However, don't lose your strength and your will during this time. It's times like these when consistent disciplinary action is essential to teaching your foster child positive and acceptable behaviours. There is no room for negotiation when it comes to bad behaviours and there should be no room for exceptions when it comes time for punishing poor behaviour.

Hopefully before any poor behaviour occurs, you've sat down with your foster child and discussed the consequences. Be concise and consistent when discussing these consequences, so that when the time to implement them comes, you can follow through with ease. Children are consistently testing the boundaries and limits set on them on a continual basis, and the temptation to 'bend the rules' just once or twice can be overwhelming when they're really trying your patience. But be firm, yet fair. Emphasize that this was the understood consequence for this particular inappropriate action, and that now is not the time to negotiate. Afterwards, take time out to discuss the situation with your foster child, and if it seems that perhaps a consequence that worked at first isn't working anymore, rethink that punishment and negotiate with your foster child. Of course, parameters that are set for their well-being or safety should never be negotiated. But in other instances, it may be time to develop a new consequence based on your foster child's age, temperament or maturity level.

It's also imperative that your partner and any other adult caregivers are all on the same page and following through on punishments with the same level of consistency and clarity. Should you determine that what was once working isn't working anymore and develop a new parameter, be sure all adult caregivers are brought into the loop so that follow-through remains consistent and clear.

NEGOTIATING THE RULES

You know as a foster carer that discussing and negotiating the rules with your foster child is never easy. Children are all very different, and what might need to be a rule for one, may not even be an issue for another. That being said, there are many parameters that you set as a foster carer that are the hard and fast rules - those with no 'wiggle room.'

Those are the rules set forth to protect your foster child's health, safety and well-being. These rules and their consequences should be very clearly defined and it should be understood by all involved that they are there for a very important reason and that they are 'all or nothing.'

Rules that keep your foster children safe are of the utmost importance. These could include everything from teaching youngsters not to touch the hot stove, to teaching your school aged child the importance of obeying the laws while riding their bicycle. Foster children need to understand that these rules are to be followed to the letter and there is no room for negotiation here.

For adolescents and teenagers, such rules should include expectations about drinking, the use of illegal drugs, etc. These rules are also essential to a foster child's health, well-being and safety. There should be no room for experimentation or relaxing the rules in specific social situations.

There are rules that can be fairly and equitably negotiated with your foster child as well. Rules regarding how many hours per week can be spent playing video games, what time a child is expected home for dinner, what time each night homework is to be completed, or how late a teenager is allowed to stay out on weekend nights are all rules that can be discussed openly and honestly between you and your foster child. These should also be consistent, however. Don't allow 11 p.m. one weekend night and then tell your teenager 9:30 p.m. the following night when going out with the same group of friends. If your teenager broke the 11 p.m. curfew the weekend before, the consequence of losing the privilege of going out that weekend should be strictly enforced. Don't bend the rule just because your teenager seems genuinely sorry and promises never to do it again. Consequences should be consistent, fair, and always followed through.

PHYSICAL PUNISHMENT?

Effective discipline does not involve physical punishment of children. Recent studies have shown a direct link between physical punishment and several negative developmental outcomes for children including physical injury, increased aggression, antisocial behaviour, difficulty adjusting as an adult and a higher tolerance towards violence. Research has also shown that physical punishment poses a risk to the safety and development of children. It is crucial for foster carers to gain an awareness of other approaches to discipline, because it is all too simple for physical punishment to turn into child abuse and result in severe physical injury, detrimental emotional damage, and even death. Each year thousands of children continue to die as a result of physical abuse.

Children have a right to be protected from physical abuse, and laws demand severe punishment for those found guilty of physically harming a child.

Foster carers must NOT use physical punishment as a form of discipline (under any circumstances).

A child that lives in an abusive environment is likely to grow up and either be abusive themselves or have severe social, emotional, physical and cognitive delays in development. Foster carers' disciplinary methods serve as strong models to children that teach them how to deal with life's day-to-day challenges. It is important for carers to model appropriate behaviour and to establish expectations as well as limits.

Children have a right to live in a safe, secure and nurturing environment, and their dignity must be respected. Carers must consistently use fair and logical consequences whenever foster children fail to follow rules. They must keep in mind that a child is not a miniature adult, and that discipline must be age-appropriate and fit the child's temperament and maturity.

Remember that a number of foster children may have experienced physical punishment and aggression from their parents, which may be why they are in foster care.

PRESENT A UNIFIED FRONT

Disciplining your foster child is never easy. You probably know from experience, and mistakes, how important it is to be consistent and firm, and to always follow through with designated disciplinary consequences. But when there are two carers involved, it's crucial they are both on the same page and apply discipline consistently.

Carers should agree on how to discipline their foster child. To become reliable to the foster child, both carers must be consistent in dealing with similar situations. If there are disagreements regarding discipline or other caring issues, they are best discussed with the child's social worker and your support worker when the child is not present. If the child senses discord, they may attempt to manipulate the situation to their advantage.

When teaching good behaviour, foster carers should "practice what they preach." Children learn values and beliefs more by the examples that adults set than by verbal instructions. Screaming at a child to be quiet is hypocritical and ineffective. Decide what is important and what response to use to teach your foster child. It would be more effective to calmly tell your foster child to be quiet or use "time-out" when a child is physically aggressive.

And remember, what works now may not work later down the road. Situations may dictate a different approach, and time and maturity may demand a rule be modified or abolished altogether. Sometimes your common sense will help you decide when bedtime rules should be modified or table manners relaxed.

Some rules will be the same, others will be modified or abolished, and new ones will be introduced. But regardless of the situation, carers should always present a unified front and work together, and not against each other, in providing effective discipline for their foster child.

Time Outs

Disciplining a young child using the time out method can be very effective, and will work with children as young as 18-24 months old. By using this method of discipline, carers are giving the foster child time to sit quietly and alone after misbehaving, without becoming angry or agitated with the child.

Designate an appropriate area in the house where your foster child is isolated from interacting with others. It can be a corner in their bedroom, a space on the kitchen floor or a special chair that's labeled specifically for time outs. The length should be age-appropriate. A good rule of thumb is generally one minute per year of age. A kitchen timer is helpful in counting down your foster child's punishment time.

Time out for toddlers is used to give them a chance to regroup and calm down. It's doubtful they will sit completely still, and they should not be forced to try.

All children should be asked in a firm, but pleasant, tone to complete a designated task or stop an undesired behaviour. If their behaviour persists, they should be verbally directed to behave once again, with eye contact being made and the time out spot pointed out. If after this warning the behaviour still persists, they should be escorted to the time out location and told exactly why they are being sent there. Maintain a calm but firm tone with them. Once they've quietly served their time in the time out location, it's important to discuss with the child why they were sent there and that if the behaviour occurs again, they will again be sent to time out.

Older children should then agree to do what you told them to do or cease misbehaving. Children who leave their time out location before their time is up must be made aware that privileges will be lost as a result.

It's likely that your time out method will have to be modified to fit the temperament of your foster child and your own parenting style. And remember to reinforce positive behaviour with praises, hugs, and smiles. Time out can successfully be used outside the home at places such as supermarkets, restaurants, or shopping centres. It's important to emphasize to the child that time out will be enforced should they misbehave while there. Be consistent and place the child in time out should they misbehave in the store. If you don't, they'll get the message early on that you're inconsistent and will be more likely to test your boundaries.

POSITIVE DISCIPLINE

Children always seem to find a way to 'push your buttons' at times and really try your patience. It's easy to feel irritated, sad, angry, annoyed, confused and hurt. It's at these times that your foster caring skills are really tested, and it's imperative that you maintain a kind, but firm, stance when it comes to implementing the discipline. And remember – don't ever hurt your foster child with physical or verbal abuse. You want to teach your foster child that such things are wrong, and punishing inappropriate action by yelling or hitting is hypocritical at best.

Your goal when disciplining your foster children is to teach them to be responsible, cooperative, kind and respectful. The best way to teach this is to always remain consistent, follow through with the same punishment for the same misbehaviour, and to discuss the discipline with your foster child openly and honestly afterwards.

Always keep in mind that the age, maturity level, and temperament of your foster child should always be considered when enforcing disciplinary action. Most importantly, remember that it's not the foster child you dislike; it's his or her chosen behaviour, action or misdeed.

If you need to, give yourself a brief 'time out' before responding with appropriate discipline. Sometimes you may need a short cooling off period before dealing with your foster children's poor behaviour in order to avoid inappropriate behaviour of your own.

As discussed earlier, yelling and hitting should never, ever be an option.
Keep an open mind as a foster carer, and be willing to learn with and from your foster child. We all make mistakes, and it's important to realise that not every form of discipline works with every child. Children are just as unique as adults are, and forms of discipline should be tailored to fit the individual needs of both foster carer and foster child. But with a little forethought, patience, firmness, love and understanding, the discipline can have a positive outcome for all involved.

TACTICS FOR TEMPER TANTRUMS

Even the best-behaved foster child has an occasional temper tantrum. A tantrum can range from whining and crying to screaming, kicking, hitting, and breath holding. They are equally common in boys and girls and usually occur from age 1 to age 3. Some children may experience regular tantrums, whereas for other children, tantrums may be rare. Some children are more prone to throwing a temper tantrum than others.

Toddlers are trying to master the world, and when they aren't able to accomplish a task, they often use one of the only tools at their disposal for venting frustration - a tantrum. There are several basic causes of tantrums that are familiar to carers everywhere: The child is seeking attention, or is tired, hungry, or uncomfortable. In addition, tantrums are often the result of children's frustration with the world. Frustration is an unavoidable part of children' lives as they learn how people, objects, and their own bodies work.

Tantrums are common during the second year of life, a time when children are acquiring language. Toddlers generally understand more than they can express. As language skills improve, tantrums tend to decrease.

Keep off-limits objects out of sight and out of reach, which will make struggles less likely to develop over them. Distract your foster child. Take advantage of your little one's short attention span by offering a replacement for the coveted object or beginning a new activity to replace the frustrating or forbidden one. And choose your battles: consider the request carefully when your foster child wants something. Is it outrageous? Maybe it isn't. Accommodate, when possible, to avoid an outburst.

Make sure your foster child isn't acting up simply because he or she isn't getting enough attention. To a child, negative attention (a carer's response to a tantrum) is better than no attention at all. Try to establish a habit of catching your foster child being good ("time in"), which means rewarding your little one with attention and praise for positive behaviour. This will teach them that acting appropriately makes you happy and proud, and they'll be anxious to do it again and again.

CHAPTER 5.

CARING FOR TEENAGERS

Everyone warns us about the terrible two's, but a toddler does not match the strife caused once children hit the terrible teens. The children in your care can change from idolizing your every move to leaving you in the dust. Everything is suddenly about them - their friends, their phone, their Facebook. Foster carers may respond by preaching nagging and threatening, often causing teens to feel less respected and becoming insolent or withdrawn. It is a never ending cycle. Though it is impossible to avoid the tug of war, you can make the days smoother with communication.

The adolescent years are naturally a time of conflict for foster carers and teenagers. It's when children grow into a distinct person. Teens naturally start pulling away, so they can make decisions independent of the mould their carers expect. What is a time of self-discovery for the teen can be a nightmare for carers. During these important formative years, carers want make sure their foster children maintain the values they have worked hard to instill. Teenagers naturally resist and argue in an attempt to assert their forming beliefs. The bumpy interaction between foster carers and foster teenagers often creates a time of confusion in the foster family. What follows are some tips for parenting foster teens. But, first let's start by understanding the mind of a teenager (as best we can!).

Gaining Perspective

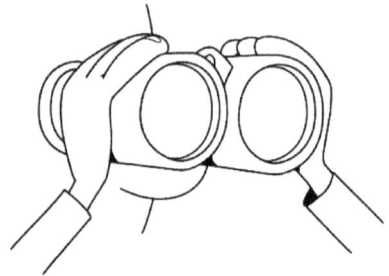

Dramatic changes in your foster child's behaviour are red flags that they have crossed into the teen years. Teenagers start to see the world in a whole new light as they start to think more rationally and abstract. They are trying to decide who they are and how they fit into the world. Hairstyles, clothing and attitudes change as they try on new identities. Children who would do anything to please their carers begin finding additional role models to fit their new image. As a result, they naturally start pushing away from their carers to be more independent. Remembering how confusing and difficult the adolescent years are can help you to adopt a healthy approach to parenting your foster teen.

Teens have a lot of issues to deal with that seem trivial to adults, but are earth shattering events for them. Remember acne, voice changes, and physical development? Your high spirited foster child may suddenly be moody for no apparent reason. At times, they don't even understand why. All of these changes are not just physical but hormonal. There are emotional ups and downs that are unavoidable. Talk to them about these changes and let them know you empathise. Teens sometimes have a hard time realizing the world is not dishing out a personal attack. Let them know you understand. Confide an appropriate story about your teen years, so they know you have been there, understand their angst and are there for them. Studies show teens with a closer bond with their carers have an overall more positive attitude.

Teens need their privacy. They are starting to form boundaries and are more sensitive to their individuality and personal space. Don't be surprised if they plaster their pastel walls with posters and other "clutter." It is their way of shedding their old selves and expressing the person they are becoming. Coming in to clean the room is the equivalent of having a spy on the loose. If it is imperative that they keep their room clean, let them be responsible for their own space. This doesn't mean you don't keep tabs on what they are doing or who they are doing it with. So, give them the respect and privacy a teen needs until they give you a reason for suspicion.

Despite teenage issues with carers, there are still times when they will need their carers help and support. Don't try to solve all of their problems. Instead, listen to their situation completely and then ask "How would you like to handle this?" Hear them out and repeat back what they said to show you respect their thoughts. Offer suggestions and if not life-threatening allow them to make the mistake. If everything works out, credit them with praise and if not be there as a support system. They will learn to handle life's problems, whilst knowing you trust and respect them as maturing individuals.

COMMUNICATION TIPS

You can't accomplish anything if no one is listening. Communication is the cornerstone for a positive relationship with your foster teen. Here are a few tips to start opening the lines of communication.

• <u>Build Trust</u>– When you give your opinion or ask your teen questions their first reaction is you don't trust them. Build trust early. Show trust by giving them some age appropriate freedoms. However, make it clear that if the trust is broken, freedoms will be taken away until the trust is rebuilt.

• <u>Practice Honesty</u>- At this age, teens develop their thinking skills. They are very aware of what you say and are sensitive to consistency. If you say one thing and do another, they will recognise your actions as two faced. By being dishonest you will lose their respect and your ability to lead.

• <u>Foster Relationships</u>- Demonstrate that their opinions matter and that you are interested in their life. Since teens are into the here and now, ask questions they find relevant. Ask them what they like to do for fun or where they may want to live after high school. A back and forth conversation helps break through the walls and build a bond the lecturing cannot break through. It's best if you don't wait until they are older to open the lines of communication. The earlier you open the lines of communication the more likely they will stay connected during the teen years.

• <u>Stay Calm</u>- Teenagers are still formulating their opinions and will take every opportunity to test their arguing skills. Avoid falling into a power struggle. Listen to their opinions even if you do not always agree with their perspective. The key is choosing battles wisely. Yelling and getting angry is an invitation for a big battle. Keep the volume down and stay calm to show you have control of the situation. They will be more likely to mirror your behaviour and have an "adult" conversation.

• <u>Spend Time</u>- Close relationships are produced by spending time together. With today's busy schedules, it can be a challenge to spend time with the family and your foster children. However, it is crucial to squeeze out regular time to spend with your foster teen and keep the lines of communication open.

Hold non-negotiable family times, and attempt to have dinner together as often as possible to ensure quality face time with your foster children.

TEENAGE TIPS

As we have established, the first step is opening the lines of communication. Once that is accomplished, you should be better equipped to deal with the everyday issues that arise. Here are a few tips to build a positive framework.

- Encourage Activities for Personal Growth- Teens maintain a better attitude when they participate in activities allowing for personal expression. Extra-curricular activities like art programs, sports or music help teens find value in themselves. Evidence has also shown teens who participate in community service engage in less risky behaviours and receive higher grades.

- <u>Allow Teens to Have a Part- time Job</u>
   It will teach them important skills for the future such as accountability, time and money management, the ability to communicate effectively and be on time. However, remember to discuss this with their Social Worker.

- <u>Build a Close Relationship</u>– Remember, communication is key. Teens are persuaded by the people they spend time with the most. By spending time, carers contribute the most powerful impact on a teen's attitude, behaviour and life approach. Form close bonds by making family dinners a time to connect. Talk to your teen about issues that are important to them such as school or their friends. Resist the urge to be a know-it-all. Instead, actively listen to their opinions and reflect what they are saying back to them so they are aware that you value their thoughts. Teens with a close bond to their carers are proven to do better academically and engage in less destructive behaviour.

- Monitor Media- According to a report by the Council of Economic Advisors teens spend 7 ½ hours each day exposed to media from tv, the internet, video games, and magazines. Teens who spend more time plugged in, are more distant from their carers. Consider restricting tv time during designated times or days and use the time to do a mutually enjoyable activity together. Use TV time to connect with your teen. Watch their favourite programme with them and after the programme is over ask their opinion about what you viewed. It is a wonderful way to hear their perspective, discuss uncomfortable issues, and teach.

- Provide structure- Teens may act unhappy when you lay down house rules. Have realistic expectations for your foster teen to meet, such as good grades, completing chores, and curfews. In reality teens understand expectations and realise that boundaries show you care about them.

- Allow Teenagers to Make Decisions- It is normal for teens to adopt their own values about life and form their own opinions. Listen to them when they have a problem and ask them how they would solve the problem. Offer guidance but allow them to make mistakes as long as it is in a safe environment. By giving teens reasonable freedom to make mistakes they can be prepared to solve future dilemmas.

- Grant Privacy– Good advice for carers is to give teens privacy. Giving them their own space shows you trust them. Though you should always know where they are going, when they are returning and with whom, although there is no reason to ask about every detail. You cannot be with your teen at all times, instead keep tabs on their activities to make sure they are safe. Respect their privacy unless they do something that makes you have to revoke those freedoms. Again, remember to discuss with their Social Worker.

• Don't Play Favourites- It is natural to have stronger feelings toward your biological children than your foster children. Just make certain those feelings do not move over to your parenting style. Teenagers are very sensitive to fairness and consistency. Treat your foster children with the same consideration and respect you do your own children. You can build a connection with the foster teen by separating your actions with your feelings until real caring develops.

• Spend Time- It is important to build a relationship with foster children that you both enjoy. Take the role of skill teacher or older friend. In this role you can play sports with them, or teach something you are good at that the teen also likes. Spend one-on-one time with them without your biological children around so you can pick up on their interests. Foster teens will probably resist these efforts at first, but over time you can build your own relationship based on mutual interests.

• Show Trust– Trust is important to teenagers. Find ways to send the message that you trust them. These concessions go a long way to a teen and will help you build a connection.

• Be a Team- It is not unusual for two people to have different ideas on how to parent children. However, teens are fighting for independence and will use signs of division to their advantage. Foster families must have a consistent message for all children. Sit down and make a plan with your partner (if you have one). Come up with a plan that works for both of you.

Foster Caring for teens can sometimes feel like walking on eggshells. But, in time a relationship built on mutual respect is possible. Remember you are likely coming into the picture after the teen has experienced many losses. You may encounter strong resistance as the outsider and should not take their displaced anger personally. However, after time you and your foster-teens can warm to each other and form a healthy foster family.

DIFFICULT TEENAGERS!

Caring for difficult teenagers usually boils down to one word, entitlement. Entitled teens think their carers owe them simply for gracing the world with their presence. These are the children who give hard working carers the silent treatment, or worse, have a hissy fit if they don't get a £100 pair of jeans. A combination of indulgent carers, the consumer culture and emotional pampering hampers some teen's ability to develop into adulthood. Self-absorbed, entitled teens are difficult to parent. However, even spoiled children can be raised as gracious and independent teens by following a few guidelines.

• <u>Limit Media</u>- Social networking such as Facebook, YouTube and Myspace encourages self-absorption and time away from the family. Hours are spent reading messages and posting the details of their lives. Some teens spend hours posting photos and descriptions of their daily activities. This self-centered focus is encouraged further by TV programs, print ads, commercials and films that promote excessive spending and value fame without talent. It has been shown that teens who spend more time with their carers, are more likely to have high self-esteem. Have designated hours when teens are allowed to watch television. Use the time away from media to do activities with the family that everyone can enjoy. Family activities take away the me, me, me's and allows teens to relate to other members of the foster family.

• Set Expectations and Consequences- Expectations have positive and negative consequences. Indulged teens don't understand how personal effort is directly connected to the outcome. Set realistic expectations and stick to a system of reward and punishment. For example, if they want something in particular make sure they complete their agreed tasks around the home. Then they will be better prepared for how the real world works.

• Encourage a Part-time Job- Spoiled children think anything they want somehow magically appears. A part-time or summer job gives teens a sense of accomplishment and earned independence. Earning their own money helps teenagers learn the value of money and appreciate their material items. They will begin to learn firsthand that anything worthwhile takes effort. Being part of the workforce will also help them to acquire life skills like punctuality, organization and working as a team that they can use as an adult.

• Encourage Volunteering – Let teens broaden their view of the world away from what only personally affects them. By volunteering they can take the focus off of themselves and help others. It will also give them an appreciation of their own circumstances by knowing there is always someone who has less. No matter what their age or abilities there is an organization where they can help out after school or on the weekends. The experience will help them develop compassion and a broader understanding of the meaning of life.

• Be Authoritative- Due to wanting to be their foster teens' friend or feelings of guilt for not spending more time with them, some foster carers may adopt permissive parenting styles. Studies show this lenient approach creates entitled character traits in teens. An authoritative parenting style creates clear boundaries for your teen. You are doing your foster teen a disservice if they are not taught life's social hierarchy. They must learn before adulthood that bullying or whining will not likely win them the big promotion.

Caring for a difficult foster teenager is a challenge if they have been indulged since childhood. For extra help, there are a number of very effective books available from Amazon to help you to care for your foster child through the tough teen years.

Chapter 6.

Raising Children Who Succeed

It is one of the most powerful things any person can do, to choose to raise a child (particularly if the child is not your own). Whether he or she is a genetically related child or one you have fostered or adopted, the commitment is huge.

There is a well-known saying that to have a child is to wear your heart forever outside your body. To some extent that is true. Think teenage angst was bad? It's nothing compared to the first time you have to deal with a child's heartbreak!

With our busy lives it is so easy to become geared up to making sure our foster children have all the essentials covered, such as food, shelter, learning to read and write, and all those important jobs done, that we forget that so much of what our foster children need us for is for us to impart a spark of desire in them to succeed, to become all they were made to be.

It's the drive of many foster carers to watch their foster child surpass them in their life in some way. Whether it is with a talent, a discovered passion, or their standard of living, foster children should be able to combine what they learn from your mistakes, and your life lessons with the lessons and opportunities they themselves face and collate them together to succeed.

To have a successful foster child we need to create a childhood that breeds success. The best part about this is it doesn't cost you thousands of pounds in private school fees or in plenty of extra-curricular activities. In fact, with just a little time, some listening and a whole lot of talking you can achieve great things!

Helping a foster child succeed in today's world is a little different than it was a few generations ago. Back then, it was considered wise to teach children to become a salary and wage earner, working in a stable job from the moment they left school until retirement. Success was measured by how long you stayed in the same job. Consistency and stability were the favoured attributes.

Then it was all about working your way up, about starting out in the business, any business and working your way up to the top, not worrying about whose toes you may step on along the way.

More recently things have changed. The more recent generations coming out of school accept they will probably have at least four to five career changes over the course of their life. They know how to flaunt their talents and sell themselves and aren't too scared to do it.

These kids, the ones who succeed today, are good at finding the gaps in the market and filling them. They'll walk away from a job that doesn't offer them a good mix of lifestyle opportunities, perks and career advancement. They often prefer to work to contract than be tied to a permanent position. Security and consistency aren't words in their employment vocabulary.

This is important to understand as you look at raising foster children. This current generation seeking employment may have different attributes than the one your foster child will be in, but it's likely to be more in line with how it will be than the generations of your parents and of yourself.
Your foster children today are growing up with a very different world view than the one we once had. They may want to be self-employed, own their own businesses, and pursue creative endeavours. While of course some children still veer to traditional roles, the majority of children feel attracted to roles that were previously seen as just for those creative types. Even jobs in IT can be incredibly interactive and creative, and children in our technological ages are attracted to them

How Do We Define Success?

Of course simply said, your foster child is a success if they grow to be healthy, happy and able to be independent of you. However, for most carers, while they say that is all that they want for their foster children, it's not all that they might expect from them.

Take a moment to look at your own life. How do you measure your own success? Is it through the type of possessions you own, the work you do, the way you live your life? Is it your relationships, your children? Think about what you feel are successes in your life and write them down.
The amazing thing about fostering is that you teach your foster children even when you don't mean to. So that list of your own successes is important. It gives you a starting point of what your foster child is already learning form you about what is important in your life, and they will follow it.

Once you have created your list read over it once more and think about how you learnt those elements of success. Put them into groups – emotional, spiritual, and physical and economics. We will look at all of these as a group, but it's important to consider them individually to begin with.

We all have different areas that we consider are the most important to measure our success in. For some, finding one person to spend the rest of your life with, raising children together, may be the pinnacle of your success. For another it may be growing a business and becoming the CEO of a Worldwide organization, and for another it may be working with a group of people who need the services of someone committing a lifetime of free work alongside them. All of these are important. All of them add to the world we live in. To create a successful foster child, you need first to recognize that success isn't just about being the richest child in the street. It's about awakening the inert dreams and hopes each one of your foster children holds inside their heart and bringing them to life. If you do this, then your foster children will succeed.

While your foster children will copy you, and follow you, they are not carbon copies of you. Even if you've come from a long line of doctors, and you yourself are one, it doesn't mean your foster child is going to be the same. Once you have worked out how you measure success and what values you want to share with your foster children through your modelling of those measures, you then need to acknowledge they are a separate person from you, and still may go a completely different route.

The precise nature of how they show their success isn't as important as how they carry out any task before them. The skills needed to run an organisation in say, a Third World country, are very similar to those of running a business or a home. It's just placing them in a different context.

To succeed, children need to be able to work with a wide range of people (have good people management and leadership skills), to be able to identify a problem and then also have an idea of how they can go about solving it. This combination is a winning success formula that can help your foster to succeed.

Foster children need your expectations and your ability to tease out of them their positive attributes, but they don't need you to carve out a specific future for them. They are able, even at a young age to do that themselves.

WHAT DON'T CHILDREN NEED

Whatever the planned end result of your foster child's success, all children start with the same needs and wants. Essentially it's the same plan to create the most successful life.

The best and most powerful thing to realise is that you can't stuff it up with one mistake. Nobody is perfect, so you are going to make mistakes You'll lose your temper, forget to watch a game, say no to something deeply important. Funnily enough it's as much your own mistakes in parenting as your successes that can contribute to your foster children's success. Your mistakes can give your foster children a point of comparison.

Most children who grow to be hugely successful often had almost dysfunctional upbringings. They may have lost a parent early on, lived in near poverty or just never fitted into school. There are many external factors that occur to children that we have no control over. And these things, instead of being a negative influence, can turn around and become part of what creates success for them. Perfection is not required.

Luxury is also not a necessary part of your foster child's success. Children who grow up in luxurious surrounds with all their physical needs met don't develop the hunger they need to go out and make it on their own. They have no need to- they've already got it.

Some very wealthy people choose to raise their children very humbly and simply to encourage them to create their own path to success.
If you provide your foster children with everything they need, and everything they want, they have no reason to solve the problem of how to get what they want. If you are familiar with the story of Charlie and the Chocolate Factory, the characters of each child except Charlie are of parents who love their children through indulgence.

If we have a lot, it feels natural to give to our foster children. However, the best gift we can impart is the gift of developing their own resourcefulness. It's a little bit more of a long term thing, but it's a powerful gift to give.

This is great news for those foster carers who worry about how a lack of finances can negatively impact their foster child. It doesn't need to. The saying, "necessity is the mother of invention" is certainly true when it comes to your foster child developing a creative and inquiring mind.

WHAT DO CHILDREN NEED

The path to your foster children's success begins right at the start. Children are not born as an empty vessel, waiting to be filled. Each one already has some innate talents, a personality that will develop and grow. If you have more than one foster child, you may know how amazing it is to watch both children grow up in the same environment but grow so differently, and respond to different things.

While your foster child is not an empty vessel, they are a little like a sponge, absorbing both the good and bad that comes their way. It's your job to create an environment that gives them a strong foundation to build their success from.

To start the foundations right, all children need an environment of good boundaries, routines, rules and responsibility. These words are often bandied about but the following sections are a basic rundown of how these work to create success.   Some of these topics have been covered earlier in the book in a different context, but here we are revisiting them in a bit more detail in terms of achieving success.

BOUNDARIES

These are not hard fences, but are rather the universal laws governing your home. The first boundary has to be love, and is best started from when your foster child first arrives with you. Your foster child's understanding of unconditional love, that you'll be there for them no matter, what begins here. If this boundary is well established everything else is easier. You need to attend to your foster child's needs, as they occur, and learn to read the personality of your foster child and adapt your parenting style to suit. Each foster child needs to be parented differently.

After love, comes consequences. Focus on natural consequences, such as tidying up a mess they've made themselves, paying for the window they broke, or apologizing face to face for a wrong they've committed. This has to be age appropriate (young children may sometimes only clean up a portion of the mess, and you help with the rest), and it needs to be

144

consistent. Everyone is allowed to have a rough day where you just sort it out yourself, but it's good to keep going with the boundaries you've created. The chief boundaries basically boil down to three important things: Respect for self, respect for others, and respect for things.

Creating good boundaries is important. As an adult we sometimes make conscious decisions to enlarge our boundaries, to allow people to walk over us a little, or sometimes we do the same to them, particularly in business. But well established boundaries help in all areas of our life from relationships to business. They help us to avoid addiction, and build positive, strong and effective relationships with others- all of which add to our success. Spend some time looking at the boundaries, the natural boundaries you have today. These are often our physical environment, our state of fitness and finances, and time to list but a few. See how these all naturally curtail us and create boundaries? Of course for huge success to happen most of us need to step outside of these boundaries at some point, but this works best if we first know where the boundaries lie, and which ones are more important (those that are relationship based for example) than others. The best thing about routines is not about the sticking to them black and white, day in and day out. The best thing is when you decide to trust your foster child to a non-routine moment. A child loves the occasional late night far more if they know it's secretly past their bedtime. Some kids may love getting pancakes on a Sunday as it means it's a different day to the rest of the week when all they had was toast or cornflakes. If every day is a haphazard day, they don't have anything to centre themselves on, and treats get all mixed into the chaos.

Set some routines in place- and let them suit both you and your foster children. Sit down with them to explain any changes and then introduce them. If you are not used to giving your foster children routines, do expect some resistance (it can feel like a lot!) and just remember to be consistent and calm while making sure those new routines get established. Some foster children will adjust easier; others will take up to three weeks to adjust. If it's a good routine (such as a regular bedtime) you may be surprised at how fast you begin to see some huge payoffs for your decision.

RULES

All rules stem from the boundaries that you've created. There doesn't need to be a lot of these, in fact it's easier to keep them as simple and as consistent as possible. Create rules that both develop a good sense of respect for self, others and things, and develop responsibility

Most of us work better if we have a little carrot in front of us. It may be money, or time off, or the longer term payoff of a better relationship. These are the things that drive us.

Rules are far more likely to be adhered to if children can see the payoff for doing so. Work out consequences for rules not being adhered to and stick to them firmly right from the start. If your foster child is consistently bucking the system, look at the rules. Does your foster child perceive its fair? Are they confused as one day you make them stick to the rules and the next day you don't? Keep it simple, keep it consistent. Sit down and work out the basic rules of your home. These can be quite broad, and relate back to the boundaries.

They may be as follows:

- Our house is a place where we talk to each other with respectful and pleasant voices.

- Our house is a place where ours and other people's belongings are cared for and we put them away when they are not in use.

- Our home needs a lot of work to make it run, and it's everyone's job to help at their own level to help it get there.

The focus on rules is to keep them positive and broad, and simple, and then let your little rules spring from these. These rules closely reflect your own values.

What rules do you already have in your home? Are they currently being enforced? If not, why not? Is it because they are far too many, far too complicated? Or is it that you yourself can't see the reason for them?

Write down the rules in your home. Take a look at them. Are these rules that will contribute to your foster child's future success? Tweak the rules until they are both something you are happy to enforce, if necessary, and something that will positively improve your foster child's chance at success.

Responsibility

In the Western world we often now raise our children to be little princes and princesses. We want them to be children, to play and have fun. If we do take away the fun, it's normally to replace it instead with extracurricular activities such as after school football, tennis or dance. While of course all of these have a place, and teach us important skills, it's often at the cost of a more important lesson – of learning responsibility.

When we get busy and find ourselves running from activity to activity, we also often move into the "I'll do it, it's easier" mode. We get them dressed, we pack their bags, we make their breakfast, or we half do their homework.

Sometimes it's good to check just how much you are doing for your foster child, and therefore preventing them from developing their own independence.

It is good to make sure your foster children have jobs and a role in your family. This is their training ground. Once used to it, they'll thrive on feeling responsible.

Identify what your foster child is currently responsible for. Ask yourself if it is age appropriate, and if it needs challenging. Are they contributing to the running of the household? A three-year-old can fill the recycling bin, a five-year-old can clean up their toys, an eight-year-old can make a salad for dinner, and a teen should be able to do some shopping if required.

Your foster children will want to succeed if they feel it's all part of being on a team. Build a sense of you all working together towards the common goal of a happy and healthy family.

 Children want to be involved- it's a natural and healthy inclination.

THE LEGACY OF BOOKS

One of the most powerful tools in creating a foster child aiming for success is to create a hunger to learn. This can be done with just a regular visit to your local library. Make it a must-have activity for your week, getting out a mix of both non-fiction and fiction books for them to read.

During the week engage them and discover what they are currently interested in and help them to find books on that topic to investigate further.
Schools do a great job in teaching our children, but successful foster children have carers who invest time in helping feed the big "why" and "how" questions that a teacher of a large group may not get to. Learning to find the answer to the big questions is a wise move on your part and helps your foster child to learn skills once again, in sourcing their own information.
Once they are old enough, Google, of course, is a wonderful search engine, but surround yourself and

your home with books first and you'll be setting up a life long journey of self-education and success.

HELICOPTER CARERS AND

COTTON WOOL KIDS

A helicopter carer is one who hovers around their foster child in case their foster child fails, or to ensure they are on their best behaviour. They are the type of carer whose foster child brings in the most amazing science projects, done mainly by the adults in the house.
Helicopter carers prevent their foster children from seeing what they can do themselves, learning to enjoy their own independence because they are doing everything for them instead.

A cotton wool kid can be the by-product of a helicopter carer or just a product of busyness. These are children who have everything done for them, often because it's easier for the carers to get ready to leave the house or get to work on time. Cotton wool kids can't develop the resourcefulness a child needs to succeed as they become too scared to try anything new.

Children are more likely to be successful if they are confident at initiating ideas, and happy in a wide range of situations. Don't be a Helicopter carer!

TEACHING SOCIAL SKILLS

It used to be that the most important attribute we were meant to have was our IQ. It was something we were born with, though of course a good education and a positive home environment does also affect IQ scores.

More recently people have looked at the Theory of Multiple Intelligences and started to value all the different ways people can be clever. A mathematician may be fantastic with numbers for example but not great at writing a literary essay, or vice versa.

It's very important to give your foster children a wide range of opportunities to discover what they are good at early on so they can decide what they want to focus on. However, one thing no one can really get away with anymore is having poor social skills.

Of course some of us are better than others at being good with people. If you've got a little chatterbox who finds it easy to smile at strangers, and interact with others, then you're sorted. However, all children need to learn to interact with people, so they can use this skill later on in life.

If you've got a shy foster child it's still important that they learn skills in communicating. Talk to them about overcoming fears, embracing fear and using it. Even children as young as five and six can understand this. If you've been nervous speaking in public, share your own experiences.

Never force your foster child into a situation where they feel unsafe, but offer to share it with them. Refuse to be curtailed by their fears however. If you are naturally exuberant and cheerful, let your foster child see the way you interact with others, rather than you opting to stay at home because new social settings make your foster child nervous.

Use a wide range of tools to help your foster child become more confident with others. You can role play with toys, and teddy bears, or make a conscious effort to invite friends over. Interact with other foster carers, and get your foster child into situations where they already enjoy themselves and feel relaxed such as a soccer team, or a drama class.

Teach them manners and help them to learn tools to self-manage difficult situations. Talking to an adult for most children can really be a last point of call.

MONEY, MONEY, MONEY

Giving your foster child a good education in money is one of the key steps to success.

Start small. Give your foster children money as part of their contribution to the team in your home. You should also give them pocket money that has no jobs attached to it as agreed with your support worker and the child's social worker.

Encourage your foster child to use the money after it has accrued a little rather than blowing it every time on sweets and lollies.

Even if you can afford it, don't buy them everything they want. Give toys and DVDs and games as rewards for hard work, or get them to work towards them by earning extra money with you.

The earlier you can teach your foster child to make money away from a salary or wage earning method the better. Talk to your foster children about passive income and provide them was ways to learn about how they can earn it.

Also consider other methods of earning for your foster child. If they are creative, they may want to design jewellery or something similar. There have been children as young as thirteen who have patented cool inventions, or become the chief designer of their own fashion label. That's a definite sign of success!

TAKE ACTION

Well, that's about it! We have looked at your roles and responsibilities when caring for somebody else's kids, and the need to strive for the best outcomes for them. We have looked at a variety of strategies for managing the multitude of challenges that you may encounter along the way. We have explored the mysterious world of teenagers and we have finished with some strategies to help your foster children to achieve lifelong success. All of these tips and advice can be very effective, but only if you implement them (consistently!). None of this is rocket science. It's mainly common sense with a sprinkling of theory and practice. This stuff really does work, but only if you use it......So, talk to your foster child's Social Worker and agree on various strategies that you are both happy with. Then Take Action! You won't regret it.

OTHER BOOKS BY DAVE CREWE

Adoption Panel – The Missing Manual

This is a Complete Guide for Adoption Panel members, offering helpful tips and advice in order to fulfil your role effectively. It covers areas such as Quality Assurance, attention to detail, and effective decision making. It is available in paperback and Kindle formats from: www.amazon.co.uk

CAN I ASK A FAVOUR?

If you enjoyed this book (I hope you did!), found it useful or otherwise then I'd really appreciate it if you would post a short review on Amazon. I do read all the reviews personally so that I can continually write what people are wanting.

If you'd like to leave a review, then please visit www.amazon.co.uk and search for the title.

Thanks for your support!

Dave Crewe

www.ingramcontent.com/pod-product-compliance
Lightning Source LLC
Chambersburg PA
CBHW071358310526
45789CB00020B/476